NAKED TRUST

Naked Trust: *Strip it All Away*

Copyright © 2019 by Eric Gilmour

All rights reserved.

"Scripture quotations taken from the New American Standard Bible® (NASB), Copyright © 1960, 1962, 1963, 1968, 1971, 1972, 1973, 1975, 1977, 1995 by The Lockman Foundation. Used by permission. www.Lockman.org"

Scripture quotations marked (NLT) are taken from the Holy Bible, New Living Translation, copyright ©1996, 2004, 2015 by Tyndale House Foundation. Used by permission of Tyndale House Publishers, Inc., Carol Stream, Illinois 60188. All rights reserved.

PULPIT TO PAGE PUBLISHING CO. BOOKS MAY BE ORDERED THROUGH BOOKSELLERS OR BY CONTACTING:
PULPIT TO PAGE || U.S.A & ABROAD
PULPITTOPAGE.COM

NAKED TRUST

STRIP IT ALL AWAY

ERIC GILMOUR

CONTENTS

"LORD, MAKE ME STILL ENOUGH SO
THAT I CAN HEAR YOU. GRANT ME
JOY SO THAT I MAY NOT
MISREPRESENT YOU. AND GIVE ME
SWEETNESS SO THAT YOU CAN KISS
YOUR PEOPLE."

———

I have found in my life that it is more important that He has my *attention* than me knowing what to do. I think that this concept works its way into every area of life. There are often situations where there is a temptation to not be yourself. But I felt like the Lord said to me that if I change who I am, I cannot accomplish the purpose for which He put me here. And I think that goes for many things in life. You are right where you are because *you are who you are*.

I feel I need to *present the Lord* in the way that He has *presented Himself* to me, it's a deep conviction that I carry. So, I can only give to you what He has given of Himself to me. I feel it is very important to say this because people ask me all the time, "Why are you so mushy, why are you so lovey when you speak about God?"

It's because every time He comes to me, He rushes in like a knight in shining armor rescuing me again, and again, and again! He comes in, and He treats me as if I'm the only one in the room. He is so kind, and He is so full of love. I'm telling you, He looks at you as if there is nobody else. You are a lily among thorns to Him, and He is captivated by you. There is nothing that brings His heart more joy than when you are captivated with Him too. These truths, when realized, begin to strip away our lives of anything that keeps us from Him.

As we begin a journey of stripping away all and entering a place of *naked trust*, pray with me:

> I COME TO YOU, OH PRECIOUS LOVE OF MINE. YOUR LIPS DRIP WITH HONEY AND YOUR KISS IS LIKE WINE. YOUR EYES ARE SO TENDER, AND YOUR VOICE IS ALWAYS KIND. YOUR TOUCH IS BLISS TO ME... I LEAVE EVERYTHING ELSE BEHIND. I'M YOURS LORD, AND YOU ARE MINE. EVERYTHING IN YOU I FIND. YOU GIVE FLIGHT TO THE BUTTERFLIES IN MY SOUL. IT'S YOU WHO SOOTHES ME

AND YOU WHO EXCITES ME. YOU SPREAD JOY LIKE RAIN INSIDE ME. LORD, EVEN WHEN I'M SHATTERED, ALL OF MY PIECES THEY FLY TO YOU. YOU ARE MOST LOVELY TO ME.

ALL THAT I'M ASKING IS THAT YOU WOULD OPEN OUR EARS TO HEAR THE SWEETNESS OF YOUR TENDER VOICE, BECAUSE IT CUTS AND IT CHANGES AND IT BUILDS AND IT LIFTS US UP TO BE WITH YOU. AMEN.

"OH, HOW OFTEN MEN HAVE
GIVEN ATTENTION TO GOD'S
GOALS RATHER THAN GOD
HIMSELF."

———

THERE IS A WORD THAT HAS REALLY BEEN IN my heart recently. It's the word "only". Such a small word, but it's very exclusive. *Only* means "there are no others." I've been feeling a song arise in my heart that says, "Only you Lord, there are no others."

I feel as if I'm like Cinderella throughout the day, letting a song go up to the One who has captivated my heart. I can feel it on the inside. I have become addicted to the way it feels when I give attention to Him. I feel as if the love that He has shown me is of such a kind that it's impossible for me to be the same way that I was before. I feel as if every touch is fulfilling me in a way that nothing else could possibly fulfill me. To say *only* is to say, "There is not a saint, not an angel, not a man, there's no one else but You." To say *Only You Lord* is to say, "There's nothing else. It's only You. Not a gift, not a promise, not a blessing: it's *only* You."

This is what I desire. I'm praying that what begins to happen in your life today is that you would be injected with an "only You, God," disposition and that you will allow nothing else, not even the stuff that He gives, to take His place. *Only You* means, "not even my wife, not even my kids, not even my friends, not even my family, no one comes close to You. You are in a category all by Yourself. My heart completely belongs to You." This is the *only*, and I believe this is what He is after. He wants an *only*.

Most people never experience Him as *all* because they never find Him as *only*. You'll only experience Him as all that you *need* when He's the only thing you *want*.

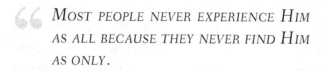

> MOST PEOPLE NEVER EXPERIENCE HIM
> AS ALL BECAUSE THEY NEVER FIND HIM
> AS ONLY.

It's all of these additions to Him that stop you from being able to experience all of Him. Oh, to only have Him and to only want Him. This is it! David writes with his poetic pen in his journal of love:

> "For who in the skies is comparable to the Lord? Who among the sons of the mighty is like the Lord, A God greatly feared in the council of the holy ones, And awesome above all those who are around Him? O Lord God of hosts, who is like You, O mighty Lord?"
>
> - PSALM 89: 6-8

―――――

AM I ENOUGH FOR YOU?

If there is *anything* that happens to you during this book, let it be a bursting love from your heart toward God. A love that, only, only, only desires Him. A love that declares He is far above even the things that surround Him. God longs to be longed for. He's seeking to be sought. And throughout all of your days He will be peering into your heart to find out if you still want *only* Him. With all the things that come to you in your life and all the things He adds to you through blessing, because He is good — He asks you again and again, in the core of your heart, "Do you still *only* want Me?" I feel as if the question that is coming out from heaven is God asking, "Am I enough for you still?"

I feel as if His heart is reaching out for each one of

us to answer this question with sincerity, "Is God really enough?" Just God. It's so important. It's going into the motives and the intentions of our hearts.

There is something that happens when He is enough. He kills competitions, comparisons and frustrations, disappointments and offenses, betrayals and hurts, bitterness and resentment, questions and unbelief. They are all solved with one simple, "Lord, You are enough for me; not just now but for eternity. I desire you Lord, and *only* You. There is nothing else."

I'm sure that you have found, and you will continue to find, that every single situation in your life, no matter the nature of it, brings you face to face with whether or not God is still enough for you.

You say, "Eric, what I'm going through has nothing to do with God." No, it has everything to do with God! "No you don't understand. People are betraying me, people are being harsh toward me, and there are situations of sin and dysfunction happening around me." Every single one of them will bring you back to face this question: is God still *enough*; is He *only*? This is what He is longing for.

We search high and low for answers and His

answer is always Him. We search high and low for answers and the answer will always simply be *Himself*. Every revelation is just Him unfolding Himself again. So you find that you hit these road blocks in your life. And when you get there you find that you are in need of a revelation. And then He comes in and He says, "It's Me. What are you looking for? Well, it's Me. If you'll understand who I am, you'll realize that you can't find anything outside of Me, everything there is, is inside of Me." God has locked Himself up in the person of Jesus Christ so that there is *nothing* of God that is accessible *outside* of Him. And everything of God is accessible only in Him. God is saying, "Am I enough? Am I enough for you?"

> *WE SEARCH HIGH AND LOW FOR ANSWERS AND HIS ANSWER IS ALWAYS HIM.*

Most of our issues are pointing back to the fact that somewhere along the way we've moved past His inexhaustible person. We find ourselves growing when each trial and each resistance brings us back down to Him, again and again and again. A singular possession; a sole focus.

He watches sovereignly over each detail of your life to be let in again as *all*. He is looking down from Heaven, seeking to and fro throughout the earth, looking for a heart that is completely His. Do you know what a heart that is completely His looks like? It's a heart that has "only You, Lord" written on it. There are no others. There are no others, Lord. It is *only You*, it has always been only You, and it will always be *only You*. This is what God is looking for, a heart that is completely His.

OUR CHOICE: OTHERS OR HIM

So, we have a choice ever and always before us. To let go of all others and to have Him, or hold on to them and be without Him. It's our choice. He won't force you; He'll wait, hoping that soon enough you will get tired and remember Him. You may be tired. And God lets that fatigue set in so that you will remember one day, "Come to Me, all who are weary and heavy-laden, and I will give you rest" (Matthew 11:28).

I pray the Lord even now begins to give you rest as you recenter your heart on only Him. See, He peers through the lattice, He reaches His hand in to try to arouse your affection for Him again. "Remember Me," He says, as He puts His hand through. He says, "Just remember Me," because in that turning of attention back to Him, the heart gets captivated again and again.

You cannot see Him and not be taken. So He

shows Himself to steal your heart away. And He does this again and again. I'm telling you many times God blocks the future from you. He conceals it so you can't see it. He does this on purpose because He is jealous to have all of your attention. Oh, how often men have given attention to God's goals rather than God Himself. Many times He'll just block it, and you will not be able to see the next step. What He is doing, is trying to make you come face to face with whether or not He is still enough for you.

He's jealous for all your attention. He will not share it. He will not even share you with the things that He has promised you. Many men have cheated on God with stuff God gave them. It's a problem. "Only You" is what we need. I ask you to let the Holy Spirit deeply search your heart and ask you this question: is God still enough?

"WHEN A MAN HAS MET GOD,
HE'S NOT LOOKING FOR
ANYTHING BECAUSE HE HAS
FOUND IT." —TOZER

———

THERE'S SOMETHING THAT INTRIGUES ME IN history: the relationship we see in the Scriptures between God and His man, or a man and his God. Nothing moves me quite like this. We have Abraham as a friend of God. Job is said by God to be like nobody else on the earth. Moses spoke with God face to face. Daniel was called a man greatly loved, and John was called the beloved. But there is a unique description, a description that moves me more than all the other ones; it's what is said of King David. He was a man *after God's own heart.*

A man's life can be summed up in a book or maybe two, but David's whole life, all that he did and accomplished was summed up in this statement: *he was a man after God's own heart.* Literally a man who longed for God, a man who longed for God only. A man whose journal reads, "My soul thirsts for You, my flesh yearns for You" (Psalm 63:1). He's literally saying, *my entire being is aching for you*. A man whose sweet intimate love exchange with God causes him to write in his journal again, "...my soul pants for You..." (Psalm 42:1). There was an audible, craving and hunger for his God.

I remember reading about John G. Lake. He felt he was so hungry for God, he would scream out on the street. So hungry for God the ache would rise up on the inside. David has this same lover's ache. We must possess this ache. Why? Because backsliding is when your heart stops aching for Jesus.

DAVID'S ATTENTION: HIM

As I mentioned above, David said, "My soul thirsts for You..." (Psalm 63:1). David is saying, "all of me needs all of You to satisfy everything inside of me." His heart was so taken with God, that many times, his logic seemed to be suspended. It's as if he was so wrapped in his God and so transfixed with his God that he was unable to be affected by people or the actual situation that he found himself in. He uttered sentiments like, "These people seek my life, men seek my life, but I'm in love with Your words" (See Psalm 54 and Psalm 119).

He seems to be so preoccupied. He doesn't deny

that things are going on, but his preoccupation with words that he calls, "sweeter than honey" (Psalm 119:103) have captivated all of his attention.

Maybe people speak falsely about you, try to frame you or say bad things about you. I'm telling you that when God's words have captivated your heart, they are sweeter than honey. There's something about the sweetness of the honey that comes from His lips that takes away all the bitterness that comes from other people's lips. Just listen to Him, hear Him. You see, David seemed to be unable to hold his attention on what was immediately going on right in front of him because of the beauty of the Lord. In David, God had found a man who was all His. David is a man who finds God as all things because God was the only thing that David wanted.

> *THERE'S SOMETHING ABOUT THE SWEETNESS OF THE HONEY THAT COMES FROM HIS LIPS THAT TAKES AWAY ALL THE BITTERNESS THAT COMES FROM OTHER PEOPLE'S LIPS.*

As A.W. Tozer said, "When a man has met God,

he's not looking for anything because he has found it." It's the secret. David pens again in his journal, "Whom have I in heaven but You? And besides You, I desire nothing on earth" (Psalm 73:25). This is David's *only You* decree. God was the only thing he wanted, and David was called the man who wanted God's heart. The entirety of this man wanted the entirety of God.

SAUL'S ATTENTION: OTHERS

You may ask, "What does it actually mean to be a man after God's own heart?" I'll go through it quickly. Looking into the origin of this statement will reveal to us exactly what it is.

Once upon a time, there was a man named Saul. 1 Samuel 10:1 says that God kissed his life and literally anointed his life through the prophet Samuel. 1 Samuel 10:6 says the Spirit of the Lord will come upon him, and he will speak for God and be changed into another man. Verse 7 says God was with him. Verse 9 says he was supernaturally endowed. He had signs and wonders, a changed heart, and he was in line with the Word of God. Verse 10 and 11 say, the Spirit of God came upon him and all the people took notice of it.

It seemed like he was God's man. God seemed to be publicly endorsing him. All the people rallied around him. In 1 Samuel 10:16, Saul doesn't even speak against people who speak against him. He literally doesn't even tell people about his position before God or the power of God at work in his life. It seems like Saul is humble. Saul who had been touched by God, refused to promote himself. In verse 21, Saul is hiding from the exaltation as king. Saul looks like he is God's man. He stood out... not just physically, but he also stood out among the people in personality and leadership. Valiant men from all over came and supported him. They rallied around him to follow and serve him.

In 1 Samuel 11:6, the Spirit of God came upon Saul mightily to deliver the people. Saul stood up in front of everyone seemingly as God's man. Saul is exalted by the people with an undeniable anointing and a demonstration of God's power that is on his life. The glory of God seemed to be on him. God was accomplishing His purposes through him. In 1 Samuel 13:4, news about Saul spread everywhere. God has a man, God has a man! Word is traveling fast that God's got His Spirit on a man. He's going to be king. He's God's extension in the earth. This is God's guy. And then 1 Samuel 13:5 comes. A host encamps against Saul, and this is where Saul begins to change.

A host encamps against him... *this* is called pressure. It's an army ten times the size of his own. Physical weapons are surrounding him. All the people are looking at him. There's commotion. He's surrounded. Everyone looks and asks, "Saul, what do we do?" The pressure is real. What you do when God is silent is the greatest revealer of what really has your affection and your attention. Saul is looking around. God is nowhere. The Word of the Lord has not arrived.

He knows that he is supposed to wait, but pressure has a way about it. It makes you start thinking about other things. So under pressure, Saul could only see his present situation. Under pressure, Saul could only see what was *right in front of him*.

So many people cry out to God for deliverance. In Hosea 11:7, God says that His people cry out to Him, but they will not adore Him. Many times it is the deliverance men seek and not God Himself. Saul waited for a little while until he saw deliverance was not coming. Which shows us that Saul wasn't waiting for God at any point. He wasn't attentive to God at all. He was thinking about the deliverance of his situation.

In other words, what Saul is testifying by not waiting is, "God you are not enough for me; I want something else from thee." Are you understanding? It isn't about merely giving your attention to what you can get, but giving your attention to the One who's worthy of it.

"...A SUSTAINED EXCLUSION
AND A CONTINUED TO LOOK
UNTO GOD."

———

PEOPLE WANT TO BE INSTANTANEOUSLY delivered out of everything, because they don't want to have to be dependent upon God every day. This happens a lot because we have to keep coming face to face with the reality of whether or not God is really enough for us.

We see that Saul did not look to the Lord. God let this host encamp against him, to expose the fact that it was not God that he wanted. He had something else in his heart. Saul's attention was elsewhere. His desires were for other things. Despite having the public appearance of being God's man, when the test came — his heart revealed something else. To only want God means the exclusion of all other things. This is what *waiting* really is. It is sustained exclusion and a continual look unto God. Waiting means that you realize that you are unable to do anything yourself. Attentiveness to God, and holding your attention there, means that you refuse to empower yourself.

It's important to understand that waiting is not your power in and of itself. The power lies in the One who has your attention. Waiting is not about waiting. Waiting is about Who you are waiting upon.

Saul waited for a little while, but his waiting was not looking at God, it was wanting deliverance. Saul waited for deliverance, but God did not have his attention. Choosing not to be attentive to God is self-sufficiency. Nothing is as opposed to God as self-sufficiency. Only God's enemies are not dependent upon Him.

Saul's impatience was ultimately an act of independence from God. Maybe Saul was disappointed in God because God didn't do something the way that Saul thought it should be done. Maybe he was disappointed with God because God didn't do it when he thought He should do it. No matter the reason, it doesn't matter, because what Saul was doing was making a statement, "You are not enough for me. I'm looking for something else from You."

Our lives testify more truly than what we say with our mouths. But to wait, to be actually attentive to God, is to testify to God, "You are enough for me. Pressure, persecution or people may come my may, but for You I wait all the day. Nothing else has my attention Lord, I only want you."

When God is enough, we are emptied of these ulterior motives, these personal ambitions, these selfish intentions, our own devices and our own desires. It means God is all that matters.

> "YOU ARE HERE, WHAT MORE COULD I WANT?"
>
> - MOTHER BASILEA SCHLINK

———

I'm trying to get to the heart of the issue. You can go lay down your life in some other country, but even if you give your body to be burned, and you don't love Jesus first, it's worthless. It has to come from a heart that is captivated with His Person and not just some fascination with our own legacy. Brother Lawrence wrote this, "I don't know what God has in store for me, but I feel so serene that it doesn't matter," (The Practice of the Presence of God).

There is a holy complacency. Complacency is generally a bad word in Christianity, but there is a *holy complacency*. You want to know what it looks like? It means to have Him is to have everything already. It means: place me wherever You wish, take me wherever You wish, say whatever You wish, I'll do whatever You wish, because as long as I have You, I have everything. You can take everything from me and give me God, I'll still have everything. You take God and give me everything and I'll have nothing.

Saul was weighed down by his own ambitions, his own determinations, his expectations, his reputation, and his need for explanations. The wonderful pressure of keeping all your attention on God is home to some and *misery* to others. Waiting strips you down to *naked trust*.

It reduces you to Him only. It is the true love that excludes everything else and leaves you with Him only. Men do not acquire faith, they are reduced to it. You can't just say, "I'm going to go get faith." No, you have to be stripped down to only Him again, and again and again. It is very important because in the midst of spirituality, we've got all these things that sneak their way in like angels of light. They present themselves on the outside as very spiritual things, but in the heart of it, Jesus is not there. It's very common. We must be reduced to Him only.

The other things that lay hidden in Saul's heart were exposed the moment that these things wanted to be lifted up above the Lord. You will come to this moment. You may have come to it already; and you will come to it again because life is one endless face to face with "Is God really enough for me?" I cannot say truthfully, "God is all I want," until He is all that I've got.

You can choose the stripping. It's called love. Have you ever seen someone get married? I remember my wife Brooke and I were at a wedding. It wasn't ours, it was someone else's. The minister said to the two getting married, "Forsaking all others, keeping only to thee." The words came out and went through me, and I felt as if God was saying, "Marry Me. Forsake all others, everything else and keep only to Me."

> *Forsaking all others, keeping only to Thee.*

God is looking for a man that He can take near to Himself. How blessed is the man that God draws near to Himself. Oh to want Him, to desire Him, to be satisfied with Him above all things. This is life itself. You don't live until He has all of your life. And it starts with the heart. We were not created for our spouses. We were not created for children or jobs or achievements or spiritual blessings. We were created for Him and Him alone. For Him to have all of the heart is what He's been after from the very beginning.

Saul couldn't experience God as all because he didn't want God as *only*. This is evident by choosing to force something to happen. When God stood still, Saul made it work. This means he wasn't interested in God. He was interested in a result, an outcome, an accomplishment. If you keep walking when God stands still, it means God does not have all of your attention. Many times God walks with you side by side, and then He just stops to see if you'll keep going... to see if your eyes are more on the goal than on Him who is with you. I told you at the very beginning, it's more important that God has all your attention than for you to know what's coming.

Saul got antsy in 1 Samuel 13:9-12. Antsiness is getting out of sync with God. Saul begins to fear the people, and this is what happens when your heart is not captivated with God. He was more aware of the people's presence than God's presence. God must be more valuable to us than our own name. Saul was thinking of his own name and his own game that he was running, and he forgot about God. Saul was *intoxicated* with his own legacy.

He forced himself to sacrifice to the Lord without the Lord. That's religion. Service to the Lord without eyes locked with the Lord is religion. This will kill you. Even the right thing without God is evil. With His presence, everything is right. Without His presence, everything is wrong. Ungodliness is everything that does not have the divine stamp on it. The stamp of God's origin is what defines something as godly.

Did you hear it from Him, did it come from relationship, or were you inspired by somebody else? Saul seeks to save his face because the more he waited, the less chance he saw for a victory. He was losing people, he was losing followers. He sought to save his face. We seek to save our face when we can't see the Savior's face. We always seek to have our eyes on ourselves for some reason. Keith Green sang, "It's so hard to see when my eyes are on me," (Make My Life a Prayer to You).

The next verse shows Samuel summing up Saul's whole behavior with one word. He says, "How foolish!" (1 Samuel 13:13 NLT). In summary, *you're a fool for not giving God all your attention.* And the very next verse, 1 Samuel 13:14, Samuel makes the statement, "The Lord has sought out for Himself a man after His own heart." There's the origin of it. Saul: anointed, touched, used, exalted, and all the while Saul had all the attention in public — David had God's attention in private. God had already sought out somebody who no one else could see. Scripture would suggest to us that while Saul's heart rose in pride in public, David bowed low in private.

God raises up those who are bowed down because when you are bowed down, you lose all desire to be raised up at all. This is the kind of thing that God loves. He's attracted to humility like this. God had found for Himself a man after His own heart in this way; one to whom God was enough. One who loved God enough to look at Him. One who loved God enough to wait for Him. One who loved God enough to be stripped down to naked trust. Such nakedness is an invitation for which God unendingly waits. To be stripped down to nothing invites God to be all. The nakedness of only wanting Him. The Scripture would suggest to us that David was plucking the strings of God's heart when no man could see. Saul had the people's attention, but David had God's attention.

> "If you have the smile of God what does it matter if you have the frown of men?"
>
> – LEONARD RAVENHILL

When We are Surrounded

God's heart was drawn to the melodies of love rising from the heart of a young shepherd boy beside still waters laying in green pastures. 1 Samuel 15:28 God says He has found someone "better" than Saul. Do you hear this language? David is better than Saul because Saul denied the Lord when a host encamped against him. But do you want to know what David did when a host encamped against him?

He's in the very same situation that Saul was in. David says, "Though a host encamp against me, my heart will not fear; Though war arise against me, in spite of this I shall be confident. One thing I have asked from the Lord, that I shall seek: That I may dwell in the house of the Lord all the days of my life, to behold the beauty of the Lord..." (Psalm 27:3-4). He's so mesmerized that his logic seems to be suspended.

War is around him and you look at David and say:

"What are we going to do? We're outnumbered, we're going to die!"

David says, "I'm confident."

"What are you confident in? Do you have another army?"

David says, "No there is only one thing I want, and it's His presence. There is only one thing that I desire, and it is to behold Him."

––––––

David is like few. It's like David says, "They see me, but I see You. Things in life are against me, but I'm leaning on You." I don't know if you've ever actually taken time to strip everything down and just simply sit with God, but if you have, you've recognized something about Him. All He's interested in doing is holding you — holding you close. David's confidence is incredible, but it's not logical. "Weapons, armies, war, I'm not worried, I only want the Lord," he says.

1 Samuel 15:12, Saul wants another chance, and he partially obeys. Then he sets up a monument to himself. You see partial obedience comes just before self-exaltation. We see that Saul's heart was not captivated by God. He wanted other things, he was out for his own name, his own kingdom, his independence. He was riddled with fear and unrest. Impatience and disobedience were all rooted in the pride that simply would not yield to God.

Oh how pride withers men into snakes and turns angels into devils. Pride is the denial of God, the invention of the devil, and the mother of condemnation. It's a flight from God's help, the gateway to hypocrisy, the fortress of devils, the source of hard heartedness, the denial of compassion, the root of blasphemy, the exaltation of self-efforts, and the spurning of God's help. Pride is the custodian of all sins. Pride will destroy you. But as Andrew Murray said, "There's nothing more humble than adoring Jesus. It puts you in your place where you belong and puts Him in His."

STRIPPED TO HIM ALONE

Saul knows that he has disobeyed, but he begins to present himself outwardly like he has been obedient. So Samuel teaches him, "Has the Lord as much delight in burnt offerings and sacrifices as in obeying the voice of the Lord?" (1 Samuel 15:22). Saul put practices over God's Person. He let the means of worship eclipse the Object of worship. Saul's love was really a love of himself. This is the root of every single *addition* to God.

We still in some way have a love for ourselves that we won't relinquish to Him and let Him strip away. A love that forsakes all and keeps only to Him. 1 Samuel 15:24, Saul is exposed, and he confesses, and then he tells the reason for his disobedience. He says it is because he feared the people and he listened to men. Fear is self-absorption. That's what it is. We will always eclipse God's voice with man's when we choose logic over listening to God.

I pray the Lord would reduce us. Reduce us down to Him alone. We cannot refuse this reduction. We have to let Him take us back down to *only* Him. We must be willing to volunteer for such naked-ness. Not only is it the state of experiential bliss, but is also the safest place there is. We must be a people radically committed to the all-sufficiency of Jesus, because every addition is a subtraction from Him.

David witnessed the dissolving of Saul while playing the harp for him. Saul was rejected because of wanting other things. David, having witnessed Saul's rejection and destruction through impatient disobedience, writes with deep convic-tion, "Wait for the Lord" (Psalm 27:14). David is saying, "I've seen what it does when you don't give God all of your attention and subject your life to loving Him and wanting Him and letting Him be enough for you. I can see it in this crazy man throwing spears at me." So he says, "Wait for the Lord...Yes, wait for the Lord" (Psalm 27:14).

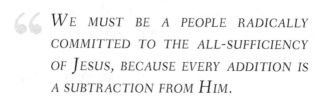

WE MUST BE A PEOPLE RADICALLY COMMITTED TO THE ALL-SUFFICIENCY OF JESUS, BECAUSE EVERY ADDITION IS A SUBTRACTION FROM HIM.

We must accept in our hearts that God does not want our *help*. He wants our *surrender*. He's not looking for elves to do His will, He's looking for conduits through whom He can flow. We must learn that prayer is better than performance. Waiting is better than work. Rest is better than running. Yielding is better than wielding. Receiving is better than retrieving. Why? Because it's in this rest and waiting that you receive God's power. And the only thing that pleases God is what God does Himself. So you receive God and God does the thing Himself. Here in this waiting place we accept the frightening inadequacy to effect God's will at all. We must be reduced to the embarrassing level of simply and only having nothing but God. *This* is the beauty. In *that place* God has no obstacle.

JACOB: DETERMINED WAITING

Do you remember the story of Jacob and Rachel? Jacob sees Rachel, she's beautiful. He wants her. So he goes to her dad, "I want her." Laban says, "Alright, I'll give her to you. Seven years of working to be able to gain her." Jacob says, "Okay."

The Bible says that he loved her so much that the seven years was like a few days. There's something about love that makes pain and discipline easy. There's something about love that links you with the reality of who and what God is really after.

The thing about this story is that Jacob is tricked by his father-in-law, and he is given Leah instead of Rachel. So now he's got the wrong girl, and he goes back. "You tricked me." The dad says, "Give me seven more years and I'll give her to you." He loves her so much that he says, "Okay." He loves her so much that he did not have contentment with just being married. He wasn't content with a person who was *like* Rachel. He wanted *exactly* Rachel.

When you love Jesus with all of your heart, you will wait for Him, because you will say, "It doesn't matter if it looks like You, it doesn't matter if it sounds like You, if it's not *exactly* You, I'm not interested. I only want You even if I have to wait 14 years, this is what I want. I want You above all things. You are enough for me."

I can see Rachel looking into the eyes of Jacob saying, "Thank you for loving me enough to wait for me." And I can see Jacob's love so deep, looking into the eyes of Rachel saying, "Time itself couldn't dampen my love for you."

This is the kind of love exchange that God wants with you. To be able to say, "Time itself, Lord, could not dampen my love for You." And God saying, "Thank you for loving Me enough to wait for Me."

I pray, *strip us down*, God, to *naked trust*. God, go into the motives and intentions of our heart, and bring us back to Your feet, where we can say, "You are more than enough for me. I have You, so I have all. You're everything to me."

———

In Luke 2:25, we're told about a man named Simeon. Simeon means "listening" or "to listen." If you think about what listening actually is, in its most basic understanding, it is literally just *attentiveness*. And if you think about what attentiveness is, it is the exclusion of all other things but the thing that you are focusing on.

So Simeon means, giving God all of your attention at the exclusion of all other things. It's living a life of listening. Simeon lived his entire life waiting for the coming of the Lord. It is this waiting, listening, and the exclusion of all other things that is the heart of what I want to continue to express in this appendix.

The Scriptures say specifically that Simeon was *waiting*. But it says firstly that the Holy Spirit was upon him. Secondly, it was revealed to him by the Holy Spirit that he would not see death before he had seen the Lord's Christ, and thirdly that he came in the Spirit to the temple.

There are three things that will accompany a life that listens to the Lord and is literally attentive to Him at the exclusion of all other things:

1. The Holy Spirit will rest upon your life.
2. The Holy Spirit will reveal. You'll have revelation from the Spirit, spiritual thoughts, spiritual words, spiritual unveilings that lead to the revelation or *are* the revelation of Jesus.
3. Your life will be quickened and moved by the Spirit.

The Holy Spirit resting on your life; the revelation that comes from the Holy Spirit, and the Holy Spirit's movement or empowerment, all come from *listening*. When living a life that gives God all of your attention, the Holy Spirit can rest upon you, move you, and reveal Jesus to you.

I believe *Simeon* is what God wants to say to you right now. And I pray that God would grant you grace to listen, to live listening, attentive to His sweet presence. And as you're attentive to His presence, in the midst of even the mundane and all the busyness of life, living listening is living in attentiveness to God.

Many times it is the additions of other things in our hearts that cause the entrance of fear, anxiety, competition, comparison, and condemnation. All of these things that come into the human soul and make a man have to fight and wrestle on the inside are normally leaked in through *inattentiveness*.

I want to encourage you, *listening* is what God is after. This is what will help you. It will place the direct contact of the Spirit upon you. I love the word "upon" because it suggests *underneath*. It suggests that something or someone is *over* you. It is subjection to God's presence. We cannot claim to be subject to God's presence if our hearts are not attentive to His Person. We are attentive to the Person of God in being attentive to the Presence. And we are attentive to the Presence in being attentive to His Person.

 WE CANNOT CLAIM TO BE SUBJECT TO GOD'S PRESENCE IF OUR HEARTS ARE NOT ATTENTIVE TO HIS PERSON.

So, I encourage you, this is yours, it's the New Covenant. No matter what's in front of you, no matter what life situation you are in, you can live *listening*.

ABOUT THE AUTHOR

Eric Gilmour is the founder of Sonship Intl. — a ministry seeking to bring the church into a deeper experience of God's presence in their daily lives. He enjoys writing on the revelation of Jesus Christ in the Scriptures and personal experience of God.

facebook.com/sonshipintl

twitter.com/sonshipintl

instagram.com/sonshipintl

youtube.com/sonshipintl

Also by Eric Gilmour:

Lovesick

How to Be Happy

Mary of Bethany

How to Prosper in Everything

The School of His Presence

Enjoying the Gospel

Into the Cloud

Nostalgia

Union

Divine Life

Burn

DISOBEDIENCE IS SIMPLY REFUSING TO LET
GOD FULFILL ALL YOUR DESIRES.

HE PLANTS KISSES LIKE SEEDS UPON MY SOUL
THAT I MAY GROW TO LOVE HIM AS HE HAS
LOVED ME.

THE LIVING CHRIST IS MOST IMPORTANT YET
MOST FORGOTTEN.

THERE IS AN INTERNAL RIVER THAT IS FLOWING
NO MATTER WHAT ANYONE IS DOING
AROUND YOU.

LORD, HELP ME TO REMEMBER THAT I NEED TO
CLING TO YOU.

Jesus, lifting my head, said, 'You cannot see Me when your head is down.'

What God has given us in the Holy Ghost is far greater than anything for which we could pay a cost.

God's works are issued out of a daily delight and joy of fellowship.

In adoration, reception begins in that definitive moment in which you can say, "Oh boy, I am in."

Without attention to His presence everything is transient.

The humble have His attention.

Two people can sit before the Lord and outwardly look exactly the same. Yet, one merely thinks while the other actually links and drinks.

Being in love makes easy the things that otherwise would be painful.

Emphasizing resistance of sin alone will never produce communion with the Spirit

BUT BRINGING PEOPLE INTO COMMUNION WITH THE SPIRIT WILL ALWAYS PRODUCE A LIFE OF VICTORY OVER SIN.

STILLNESS IS THE STATE OF BEING IN WHICH ONE CAN EXPERIENCE GOD.

MAY YOUR HEART BE CAPTIVATED AGAIN AND AGAIN. TRUSTING IN HIM IS BETTER THAN TRUSTING HIM FOR SOMETHING.

ABRAHAM'S FAITH WAS BASED ON EXPERIENCE. MOSES, THE PROPHETS, PAUL, THE DISCIPLES... EXPERIENCE IS THE SOURCE OF LIVING FAITH. IT IS A SUBSTANCE AND CONVICTION THAT GIVES UNDERSTANDING.

JESUS SAYS, "STAY AWAKE." HE IS SAYING — LIVE YOUR ENTIRE LIFE THOUGH THE EMPOWERMENT OF THE CONSCIOUS PRESENCE OF GOD.

HE HAS MADE HIS FACE UNLIMITEDLY AVAILABLE FOR YOU.

JOY IS MUCH MORE THAN AN ADOPTED ATTITUDE. IT IS THE INTERNAL PRESENCE OF THE SPIRIT.

ADMINISTRATION IS NOT A SECONDARY GIFT OF THE SPIRIT. IT IS THE VERY MEANS BY WHICH GOD MAXIMIZES AND SUSTAINS HIS WORKS. ADMINISTRATORS ARE THE STEWARDS OF PERPETUATION.

I CAN ONLY PRESENT HIM IN THE WAY HE HAS PRESENTED HIMSELF TO ME.

ADVICE: NEVER PRESENT JESUS IN A WAY THAT IS NOT IN KEEPING WITH THE WAY HE HAS PRESENTED HIMSELF TO YOU.

PRIDE AND BRIDE NEVER MIX.

OH LORD, MAKE ME YOUR LIPS.

IN TIMES OF DIFFICULTY AND FAILURE HE DOESN'T ABANDON YOU. HE KNOWS THAT YOU NEED HELP, AND HE OFFERS HIMSELF TO YOU AS THAT AID.

THE REASON HE GIVES A PUBLIC TOUCH IS TO DRAW YOU TO A PRIVATE KISS.

HE IS GREATER THAN HIS GIFTS! HE IS MORE WONDERFUL THAN HIS WONDERS! STARE AT HIM FOR HE IS GREATER THAN THE ANOINTING. HE IS LOVELY.

Only if He is center can He be source. If He is not center, He is not source, and if He is not source — something else is!

It's easy to cheat on God with the stuff God gave you.

Mary of Bethany shows us that she would rather move Him than understand Him. She was more interested in touching Him than defining Him.

We begin to suffer in various ways the moment we lose touch with His tender heart towards us.

The saving factor of receiving the Living Voice is the work it performs in the heart, far more than the specifics of information and instruction.

Rest is the submission of the soul to the Spirit's leading and empowerment.

Idolatry is what we do when we decide that we do not want to wait anymore.

Receiving life through Christ is

RECEIVING THE ABILITY TO PERCEIVE GOD'S
VOICE AND PRESENCE.

DELIGHT IS THE REPRODUCTION GROUND FOR
ALL OF GOD'S WORKS.

NOTES

_____

_____

_____

_____

_____

_____

_____

_____

_____

_____

_____

_____